Being with a Man Who Can't Drive

Being with a Man Who Can't Drive

Prophetess Twanda Pugh

BEING WITH A MAN WHO CAN'T DRIVE

Scripture quotations marked KJV are from the Holy Bible, King James Version (Authorized Version). First published in 1611. Quoted from the KJV Classic Reference Bible, Copyright © 1983 by The Zondervan Corporation.

iUniverse books may be ordered through booksellers or by contacting:

iUniverse
1663 Liberty Drive
Bloomington, IN 47403
www.iuniverse.com
1-800-Authors (1-800-288-4677)

ISBN: 978-1-4917-6974-4 (sc)
ISBN: 978-1-4917-6975-1 (e)

Print information available on the last page.

iUniverse rev. date: 06/17/2015

Contents

Being with a Man Who Can't Drive

A woman should be a jewel to a man as she is to God. She is as precious as a ruby. She is strength to her husband and a nurturer to her children. She is the key to the success of any prosperity for her husband. She is priceless. Proverbs 18:22 KJV declares, "A man that findeth a wife; finds a good thing then obtains favor of the Lord." First, the woman has to be found. Second, she needs to be ready to be that good thing in his life. Finally, the man will obtain favor of the Lord. All men and women want the favor of God to be poured on them. A woman is the one who has the ability to "birth out." God gave her the womb; this includes the fact he gave her pushing power. This fact gives her the ability to have endurance to stand with her husband. Often during the journey we wonder if we are married to whom God chose for us. God loves us so much he gave us free will and still helps us along the way.

As saved women, there are supposed to be standards that are set and followed. Yet we may sometimes feel God's way is too hard or simply too long of a process. We seem to keep making ungodly choices as women of God. How is it that we proclaim to be women of God but not women of standard? There was a time when we valued the Word of God and applied it to our lives. Now in this day and time, we do the opposite: we value other people's opinions and ignore the Word of God. However, we feel happy and content within ourselves, making our own choices. We create ways to get men instead of doing it God's way. For instance, we get on websites and let a computer match us up with men. The computer does not discern spirits; it only repeats what's been entered into it. The computer does not know when one is not being honest. What protection do we have getting a man without God? Then we have the nerve to create a program called "Sleep and Save"—sleep with him now and try get him saved later. The Word of God declares, "Be not unevenly yoked."(2 Cor 6:14 KJV)We know this, and yet we have the audacity to blame God when our relationships become shipwrecked.

I would like to minister to you one-on-one. If I may, I would like to compare a woman to a car and show you the similarities. A car is designed to carry us to our destinations; it has the ability to last a long time and endure hardship. It can sometimes be mistreated and pushed to the limit. A car needs to be serviced from time to time. The car has storage in it to hold tools that we may later need, but the space is sometimes misused and filled with a bunch of unwanted things. The tires on the car may be worn, and we have to be careful not have a blowout. The car has mirrors on the outside to allow us to see what is behind us or approaching us, but we have to glance and focus on what's ahead of us. A car has a steering wheel to lead the car where it is going and a gas tank to assist the car to go further in life. The radio inside can be peaceful to hear, or it can be chaotic. The temperature gauge in the car allows us to know if it is overheating. The motor is the heart of the car and allows it to run.

In contrast, our cars are our lives: our families, ministries, finances, emotions, and destinations. Our tires are our journeys in life, the places we must tread and go. Our trunks hold our emotions in because we chose not to deal with them. The mirrors on our cars allow us to see grace on one side and mercy on the other, and even when the enemy is approaching, we rest in God because he covers us. The review mirror on the inside allows us to glance at the past but focus on the future. Some people look at the test but focus on the testimony. The radio represents the different emotional decisions we have made because we were not tuned in to the will of God. The steering wheel represents God, who has the ability and power to drive us to the next place in him. The gas tank is the Holy Ghost filling us up to be able to follow God to where he is taking us. The temperature gauge gives us choices to be hot or cold with God; either we trust and believe him or we don't, but we can't be indecisive. The motor holds the oil that God gives us to keep us full in him.

The car has two wheels on the passenger side and two wheels on the driver side, and it takes all four wheels to move the car. The only way the car can move effectively is to have all four wheels move at the same time. How can two walk together unless they agree? It takes unity to move a marriage in a positive direction. Likewise, there are two headlights in front of the car. There is one headlight on the driver side and one headlight on the passenger side, and both headlights were designed to work together. However, if the one of the headlights blows out, the other headlight has to still shine so the car can make it to where it is going without a wreck. Compare that to a marriage: when one loses his or her light, the other one must shine so the partner can find his or her way. The husband is clearly the driver, and the wife is the passenger of this car. His job is to hear God and lead the family to destiny. The wife is the passenger, and her job is to use the Word as the road map and help her husband by giving him God's Word.

However, the driver has two qualifications for driving such a precious car. The valid driver God has chosen to operate the vehicle must be able drive you to where you need to be in God. He has to have insurance and assurance that he can take care of you. He has to have knowledge of the car he will be driving. The driver is called a husband who is validated and licensed by God himself. Can this man drive his wife to where she needs to be, or does he struggle because he can't drive?

There is nothing like being in a car with a man who can't drive!

THOUGHT PAGE

THOUGHT PAGE

Can't Test-Drive Me

When a man looks for a new car, he test-drives it to see how it runs. He wants to know what the car will cost him. In the spirit world, he is not permitted to test-drive a woman. He cannot see what your seats feel like or what's in your trunk. You are too grown to keep playing house with men because you don't want to be alone. How is it that you let a man get inside your car (your world) and drive without a valid driver's license? He is not ordained for your life. Perhaps you saw him as a Mercedes Benz: he looked good and smelled good. He had nice rims (shoes), and the interior was remarkable, but when you mentioned God, you found out his car was missing the steering wheel (God). And yet you still stayed with him, and it took a good while before you discovered the relationship was going absolutely nowhere because the car didn't have any gas. If the man was missing a steering wheel, you knew he didn't have any gas (Holy Ghost).

The Mercedes Benz with his fine and sexy self has worn out, and you are spiritually drained. When reflecting on the BMW you saw a month before choosing the Mercedes, you remember the few scratches it had on it, but it had a full tank of gas and a steering wheel. The BMW had God and was full of the Holy Ghost. He was on fire for the Lord, and every time you went to church, your spirit would leap when you saw him. But you dared not approach the man of God. Those scratches and the dent were letting you know he had been through something and that God brought him out of it. In spite of this and how his outside looked, he was still being used by God. He had a valid driver's license to drive you and your family. The BMW you turned your nose up at was a **B**lessed **M**an **W**orking in the kingdom of God.

Eventually, because of your emotions you begin to think you can change the man, trying whatever it takes to get him to submit to what you want. Finally you have had enough and move on to the next man, and then the next man. In these emotional decisions, your radio on the inside is playing louder and louder, causing you to be test-driven by different men. Now your car is being run down. The children are confused, your finances are drained, and your ministry is at a standstill. Now you are angry with God because of your free will. You were giving yourself to different drivers (men) who belonged to other cars.

You have spent so much time auditioning for a position. How can you say that, prophetess? When you do leg ministry with a man who is not your husband, you open up doors to your church. Otherwise you invite spirits in you can't handle. Then you are cooking his food, ironing his clothes, and handling his affairs—and you are not his wife. You are just another key he has to a car that is not legally his. Dealing with these types of men can cause your motor to malfunction. Your engine light is on because you are hurt, because you have spent too much time proving you are worthy to him. All the time invested cannot be gained back. You have to own up to your mistakes and move forward.

One thing women often struggle with is accepting the fact that we were used and driven in circles because of the men we chose. Anytime you are in a relationship and it is not going anywhere, look at the driver you chose really closely; see if he has a steering wheel, and check the gas gauge. Is he saved and filled with the Holy Ghost?

You may ask, "What if I was married to a minister or teacher? Does that make him valid to drive me?" The fact is you are married, but the question still remains: is it God's will or your will? Did God validate him to drive your car, or did you call him to drive you? When you are at a standstill with your marriage and it is validated by God, you are simply being serviced. Be patient as God deals with your driver (husband); trust that God will take control. Put the car in cruise control, and let God drive.

Overall, you have to remain in the Spirit of God and not in the flesh. You are not to be test-driven by different men. You are not the only woman who has been test-driven, and many of them have been saved. We women hide in the dark when we've been hurt, ashamed by a relationship or a marriage that is messed up. We begin to look for ways to show the last man that he is not the only man on earth. We don't realize at the time that we are creating a negative atmosphere out of our emotions. These emotions cause us to be test-driven by illegal drivers.

Married women don't have a right to be driven by different drivers. "Test-drive me; my husband won't know." Yes, he will know, because he will remember how he adjusted his seat. If God chose your driver, be patient while he figures out the next destination to take you and your family.

THOUGHT PAGE

THOUGHT PAGE

The Dummy in the Trunk

Every new car comes with a spare tire in the trunk. It is hidden or unnoticeable. Some people call this tire simply a "spare" or a "dummy." Which one are you?—because both words are insulting to real women. In the church today, some women think it is okay to be the other woman, especially to a pastor who is already married.

May I explain the difference between a dummy tire and the original tire? The original tire has the ability to be steady and maintain the car's balance. In contrast, the dummy tire will cause a car to ride roughly or in an unbalanced manner. The original tire will ride until something bad happens, but it waits to be restored. The dummy tire is convinced that it will not be temporary.

Let the angels assigned to our lives mount up with their wings and cover us as we are transported to the presence of God." The husband puts the car on cruise control so that God can drive, as the original plan of God is being put back in place; the dummy is no longer needed.

My sister, listen to me: everything God made is good. You do not have to settle for being a dummy for any man. You pick yourself up and become restored by God. It is not easy to accept the fact that you have been used for a man's seasonal emotions. The first thing is repentance and then restoration. When you repent, it needs to be from the heart. You can't go back to being a dummy in a new trunk. Often you must rethink your priorities in life. At the end of the day, you desire to be loved and not used.

> Now concerning the things whereof ye wrote unto me: *It is* good for a man not to touch a woman. Nevertheless, *to avoid* fornication, let every man have his *own wife, and let every woman have her own husband. Let the husband render unto the wife due benevolence*: and likewise also the

wife unto the husband. (1 Cor. 7:1–3 KJV; emphasis added)

To the Wife

Due to the fact that the dummy may confront you, there is a consequence to the driver; it depends on whether he is going to get his license suspended (separated). However, this may mean he will move out. Sometimes separation is good, but as a woman your mind will tell you he is going to go and put the dummy back on the car. That is not always true. You have to remember that you chose to suspend him, not to revoke him indefinitely. During this time in your life, you must find out what type of woman you are and where you are in God. We all know the Scripture: love covers a multitude of sin. But in your emotions you are not thinking about the Bible or God. At this point in your life, you have to decide whether you going to forgive him. If you revoke his license to your life (divorce him) and don't forgive him, then you might as well stayed married to him, because if he still lives in your mind and in your heart, and every emotion is about him; then you should not have divorced him.

Adultery is one of the most painful experiences that a woman or a man can have. It brings all kinds of emotions such as anger, bitterness, shame, hurt, fear, brokenness, low self-esteem, and rage. When emotions are all over the place, it causes the car to become unstable to ride in and is unhealthy for everyone involved. The one who commits adultery may have emotions too, such as guilt, shame, loss, and fear. I know your question: "If he is saved and full of the Holy Ghost, then how could he do this to me?" Unfortunately, he may not have had the fear of God. One thing we must remember is that God gave us all free will, and he does not take it away. In any situation the fear of God will make us not do crazy stuff. The Holy Ghost could have told him, "Don't do it, son," but because of his emotions he simply ignored the Spirit of God. But when you fear God, you are afraid to do what you want to because you know he sees everything.

Just as the dummy was in the trunk, there are tools in there as well. Use the tools to regain your momentum in your life. Lay all your issues on the altar. Be the one to call AAA (angels of war, angels of peace, and angels of God). Tell the angels to take you to the king, and be honest. Let your prayer not be in a mist; tell God exactly what you want and put your war clothes on to fight in the Spirit.

> *For the weapons of our warfare are not carnal, but mighty through God to the pulling down of strong holds;) 10:5 Casting down imaginations, and every high thing that exalteth itself against the knowledge of God, and bringing into captivity every thought to the obedience of Christ. (2 Cor. 10:4–5)*

This natural war just became spiritual, and you can't lose the battle with the Word of God. Your imagination will cause you to be in a standstill state if you allow it. You will be in a place where you will never trust again if you don't cast down your imagination. The enemy would love for you not to forgive and to stay bitter, because if you are so busy being bitter, then you can never complete the work of God. The enemy's plan is to crush your world and have you sit in the car going absolutely nowhere; you do not have a driver because he is suspended. Although the steering wheel is there and the gas tank is full, you can't take yourself to the next place in God. Therefore the motor is running and you are revving the engine, but you are stuck in unforgiveness. This will cause you to be unable to go far in your ministry. The children will lack, finances will lack, and your ministry is not where it needs to be because you are not focused due to your emotions. The motor will overheat if it continue to sit there running without being driven. Don't allow your dream to die because you will not forgive.

Divorce rates are high in society today, and it's not all about adultery. That dummy in the trunk can also be other things such as, money, bringing people in your business, selfishness, or simply taking others for granted. Nevertheless, marriages are loved by God in spite of our own way of thinking and handling situations. It is amazing how selfish we can be—for instance, hiding money from one another. We give the devil the power he needs to come back and destroy us. Some of us can be so in love with ourselves that we really have no room to love nobody else. This is an example of junk that is in the trunk.

In conclusion, we must not come out our place in God regardless of our mistakes. Some of us need to clearly clean out our trunk. Don't allow the devil to snatch our dreams or play with our emotions. We are daughters of the most high.

Encouragement to the Dummy in the Trunk

You may have been the dummy for a man before, but remember Rahab in the Bible was a prostitute who was delivered. Not only did she get delivered, she also got blessed. God spared her house because she obeyed a word that was given to her. This event in your life that brought shame is now your testimony that will bring deliverance to many others. Only when we repent can we be restored. Maybe he left his wife for you, but it will always play in your mind how you took him from somebody else. What security do you have that he will not do the same to you? There will never be 100 percent peace in your life, knowing how you obtain this man. This is why God is so important in your life: he is a restorer to all of us who will receive him. Simply pick yourself up and move forward; forget those things that are behind you and press toward the mark of the high calling. Old things have passed away—behold all things are made new. You can do this! God bless you!

THOUGHT PAGE

THOUGHT PAGE

Passenger-Seat Driver, Sit Back and Ride

Have you ever ridden in the car with someone, and you were pressing your feet against the floorboard as if you had brakes on your side of the car? Even though you know you do not have the ability to make the car stop, you still press on the imaginary brake to feel that you can change the situation. In the Spirit we do the same thing, pressing on brakes for things which we have no control over.

When God hands your husband a valid driver's license and you have to submit yourself to him, you must learn to trust him to lead you, because in actuality you trust the God in him. There are some women who are so independent that when a man comes into their lives, they don't want to turn over the steering wheel and let him drive. In the midst of the battle that they may have within themselves, they refuse to completely let go of their independence. Perhaps they are afraid of submission or need independence as a security blanket. Sometimes a woman is afraid of losing herself in a man, and so she fights against the promise of God.

Consequently, as women we get the word *submission* twisted. We get it wrong because of the mindset we have. There are things that have been taught from our parents, religion, or tradition, and because of one or the other we believe that if we submit to a man, then he will control us. Sarah loved Abraham so much that she called him lord with a lowercase *L*. It's okay to love your husband, but you cannot love him more than God. The Bible is clear on how jealous God is. According to Exodus 34:14 KJV, "For thou shalt worship no other god: for the LORD, whose name *is* Jealous, *is* a jealous God." This scripture is not some cliché—it's real.

You can love your husband without making him an idol. How do you make your husband an idol? One, by setting him above God by being more concerned with what's going on with him than you are about your prayer life. Often when we get married, we stop praying the way we used to. In a sense, we lose ourselves in that man. Everything we do revolves around him, and we are no longer interested in God like we used to be. Somehow the devil has tricked us to believe that God understands that we have a husband. God is a jealous God and not a respecter of persons. He yoked us up to work in his kingdom, not just for selfish pleasure.

For the reasons listed above, some women are afraid of submission due to the fear of loving too hard and losing themselves in a husband. On the other hand, there are good ways to lose yourself in your husband. For instance, when you make love to your husband, it is okay to give him all of you. It's fine to exhale in his arms, let your hair down, and let the moment be about you and him. That is a form of worship to God. You are with the man he ordained, and you are not shacking up. The main thing God wants from you is to keep the communication open with him, like you did before you got married.

Because submission is required when you are the passenger, you must clearly understand that it does not take away your rights of freedom. You can still communicate with the driver, but presentation is everything. You have to lose that "I am an independent woman" spirit because in fact women are the weaker vessel. For example, we go to work and permit an able body to lie in the house and do nothing. That is our fault, but we have a man of God who knows how to lead, so why not let him? The Bible declares, "Wives, submit yourselves unto your own husbands, as unto the Lord, For the husband is the head of the wife, even as Christ is the head of the church: and he is the saviour of the body" (Eph. 5:22–23 KJV). Submission allows the man to protect and care for his wife the way God wants him to. Otherwise the wife has to put her hands up and surrender because with her hands in the air, she cannot touch things she ought not to. It does not make her a door mat or stupid; it makes her please God.

In addition, as a wife you cannot use your body as a weapon to make him submit to you. The intimacy is created for marriage, not as a form of prostitution. For instance, say he will not buy you a ring you want, and then you tell him no sex for a month. Then about two weeks later he can't take it anymore so he buys the ring, and later that night you give him sex. You sold it to him—you did not give it to him. This kind of behavior is not pleasing to God because your body is not your own, and neither is your husband's. To use sex is mind control and witchcraft. When you are doing this, you might as well pull out your black hat and your broom, because you are acting like a witch and not the daughter of God. Turn away from this kind of behavior and repent to your husband and to God.

However, we can't forget about those drivers who are out of place. This is when the passenger has to pray like never before. It is just like in the natural when we know we about to wreck: we close our eyes tight and call on the name of Jesus, and Jesus comes and turns the situation around. Likewise, a marriage may be about to wreck, and that's why God suspends the husband's license so that he can deal with him. But as the passenger, the eyes must shut, with knees on the floor and body bowed; the mouth must open and call on Jesus. "Lord, restore him, get him back on track, make him strong and pleasing to you." Then you simply lay back and watch God because while he is suspended, God is still driving. When you pray for him, also pray that God changes you. God will not change him and leave you with the same mindset that your husband will never change. Prayer changes everything you apply it to, if it is God's will.

Given these facts, submission is clearly letting go of some stuff and letting your husband lead. Although it can be scary, trust the God in him. When things are not going well, prayer is the key. You don't throw your marriage way—you add to it. Where your husband has fallen short, you love him to a place of wholeness; where he is good, praise him for it. In order to be successful with submission, you cannot listen to outsiders, and you must get rid of negative phrases such as "He just stupid; he gets on my nerves; he doesn't know anything; he doesn't know how to do anything; he is worthless." These phrases will tear down your house. The Bible declares a wise woman builds her house, but a foolish woman tears it down with her hands. At the end of the day, a man wants a woman, not a woman who wants to be the man *and* the woman in the relationship. Never invest in something you don't trust, because without trust in anyone, you will never have peace.

Shut up and let the husband drive! Just because he doesn't do it your way does not mean you qualify for a new driver. Where is the oil from the motor? Isn't it still flowing in prayer, fasting, and supplication? Doesn't it still walk in love and the fruit of God? Wasn't he the one who picked you up when you were broken down on the side of the road? Does God make mistakes in his match making? Absolutely not! He is the one who calls marriages and validates the drivers of our cars. The Lord wants you to trust him more than you trust anyone. He knows what he is doing concerning your life. According to God's Word in the book of Jeremiah 29:11, "For I know the thoughts that I think toward you, saith the LORD, thoughts of peace, and not of evil, to give you an expected end. " (KJV). God's plan is already laid out; all you have to do is trust him to lead you and your husband.

THOUGHT PAGE

THOUGHT PAGE

_____

_____

_____

_____

_____

_____

_____

_____

_____

_____

_____

_____

_____

_____

_____

_____

_____

_____

_____

_____

How Do I Know He's the Valid Driver to Be in My Life?

A frequent question that you may ask yourself is, "How do I know if the man I married is the man who is supposed to be in my life?" First, you have to make sure he is sent by God, because when you are lonely you can make unwise decisions. The voice of God is important when making a life-changing decision. A woman who knows the voice of God will know not only in her heart but in her spirit. "God dances with you, and he will allow the right man to interrupt the dance and dance with you if he approves of him" (Apostle Pugh 2014).

The Word of God declares, "Be not unevenly yoked."(2 Cor 6:14) Therefore you have to make sure your decision for a mate is of God. In this day and time, we see so many people ending up in uncalled marriages. Sadly, some people live miserably for the sake of not walking in shame. The Church is not supposed to date the world, but it's happening every day. The Word is not only to be read, it is to be applied to our lives. Yes, there are a lot of dos and don'ts in the Bible, but you must have discernment. Discernment knows good from evil, right from wrong. Being with someone because another human being wants you to be is not what God wants for your life; because you will be so busy pleasing a man that you can't please God.

Another aspect to consider is whether the driver (man) is trying to drive under suspension. To be suspended means he has done some unpleasing things to God. Perhaps he cheated or was beating his wife, or he just had issues that put a strain on his marriage. However, to be suspended is to be separated from his driving privileges (separated from his wife). It does not mean that God will not restore his marriage. Therefore, he does not have the right to drive another woman. Then there is the question of why so many women love married men, and why saved women are sleeping with their sisters' husbands in Christ. The answer is simple: loneliness and no fear of God. In some cases when a man is suspended from his wife, it does not always mean he was the one who messed up. It could mean that God is working on him to accept whatever changes that are getting ready to come into his life, good or bad. Consequently, it does not give another woman the right to let him drive her family around. He is suspended but not revoked. A woman can never have him completely to herself by obtaining him the wrong way. Women look at a man and swear that his wife has done him wrong. For instance, an acquaintance of the couple has misjudged their situation and then passes on false information. In addition, she positions herself to be ready if he "needs" her. This man is vulnerable and open to the devil if he has no self-control. If indeed he has the Holy Ghost, he will not use the dummy to try to heal his emotions; rather, he will wait on the Lord to speak to him.

Although a man can be suspended (separated from his family), he can be restored. However, if that man is revoked (divorced) and then he is saved, he still must be cleared by God to drive again. Once a man becomes single and women find out, especially in the church, it is so strange. Every woman declares, "God said that he is my husband." This man is still hurt and broken. How is it that God is so clear on his word that he will let the lustful women and the broken men come together?

The fact is that good men are out there, but you have to make sure a man is sent and validated by God and not by your emotions. For that reason, you must close the door and heal from past experiences. The man has to find you, and he cannot be suspended or revoked. In order to be found by who God has in store for you, you need to be found doing the work of God, because spirit knows spirit.

A man cannot lead you if he does not have the Spirit of God. For example, imagine yourself sitting in the car, and you have the children buckled in and ready to go. You are sitting in the driveway and waiting for the driver to take off. After twenty years, you realize that he can't drive because he does not have a steering wheel (God). In your mind and spirit, you have been so frustrated for years. Then it hits you that he was not saved when you married him. Over the years your ministry has been in the same place, and you have not reached the place you need to be in God. What you didn't realize is that you spent so much time complaining that you did not ask God to give him a steering wheel. Therefore the little gas in the tank came from the Holy Ghost in you. The heart (motor) of your car is leaking oil because you are frustrated, broken, and confused. Because your oil is leaking out all over the place, you can't pray like you used to, and your worship has depleted. Because of what you've chosen for your life, you look over at your driver with disgust. Here is a common question: did you marry him for love, money, or sex? Clearly, it was not for God, because the man is not saved.

The devil is so clever about getting what he wants, and he plays on the emotions of women. One thing he wants is to destroy the destiny God has purposed for your life. The first thing you have to do is be honest with yourself. Ask yourself questions that you are afraid to analyze, such as; did I love him when I married him? Did I marry him because I was financially messed up? Or was it the premarital sex? The devil will convince you that it was God, but God is not a God of confusion. God did ordain Adam and Eve's marriage, and there was no premarital sex.

The devil knows that sexual sin is on the rise in the church, as well as around the world, and he uses it to gain more people's souls. This is the reason divorce is on the rise. The people of God have lost self-control, and as a result they have given in to their flesh. The flesh is controlling people to do sexual acts that are not permitted for unmarried people. For that reason, souls are being tied together. The Bible declares,

> What? know ye not that he which is joined to an harlot is one body? for two, saith he, shall be one flesh. But he that is joined unto the Lord is one spirit. Flee fornication. Every sin that a man doeth is without the body; but he that committeth fornication sinneth against his own body. What? know ye not that your body is the temple of the Holy Ghost which is in you, which ye have of God, and ye are not your own? (1 Cor. 6:16–19 KJV)

The scripture makes it plain that one picks up a soul tie when he or she lies down with one who is not a spouse. Soul ties keep us bound to people from whom we want to be free. Soul ties to past relationships can cause a woman to make a quick and unwise decision when entering a new relationship. She may enter in a new relationship, but she brings the people from her old life with her. Because she is still emotionally attached to the past, she is not free to move on, even though she wants to. The soul ties she has keeps her loving another man completely. She cannot love another man with all she has to give, because the soul ties prevent her from doing so.

Consequently, premarital sex has messed up many marriages. Premarital sex will cause a woman to act a fool if she is rejected after giving herself to a man. Sex is clearly designed for married people, but everyone is doing it. Sex has become a reason some people hurry up and get married. The Bible declares that if you cannot contain your flesh, it is better to marry than to burn. To marry only for sex can cause an individual to be miserable or to think sex will fix every situation. When this type of scenario takes place, the person will be married to the genitals, not the person. Everything is surrounded by sex and emotions, and there is no real love involved. For instance, when we marry out of sexual desire, we make emotional decisions right after sex, such as letting men drive our cars without licenses, giving them money, not caring if they works or not, and letting them play video games all day—as long as we know we can have sex when we get home. Emotions have caused us to miss God. The Word declares that a man who doesn't work is a man who doesn't eat (2 Thess. 3:10). This means he needs a job other than lying with a woman who is not his wife. You may not agree with what I am about to say, but I'm going to say it anyway. Prostitution is clearly giving an exchange for money or things. If he gives sex for you letting him drive your car, giving him money, or buying him games, then it is prostitution. For we who are in relationships, the Bible does not edify or solidify relationships with boyfriends and girlfriends. God ordained husband and wife relationships. The only other type of relationship in the Bible between a man and a woman is between a harlot (prostitute) and a man. Then we justify our sin by using phrases of the world such as "common-law marriage." The devil has fooled some people. We forget common sense and break the law!

Ladies, if you are married, ask yourself why you married him—and be honest with yourself. If you are shacking up with a man, make him honor you by marrying you because he loves you and not because the milk is free. Make sure all soul ties are broken and every door to the past is closed tight. Make sure you allow God to teach you how to be a wife so that you are mentally, emotionally, and spiritually ready to be married. Walk as the daughter of God and not as a worldly woman. Being ready for marriage means that you have to be ready to submit to your driver; you will read about submission in another chapter. You will know: if he loves and fears God, he honors you, and he is concerned about you spiritually, emotionally, and physically. Marriage is when he treats you as a ruby, you treat him as the king he was purposed to be, and the both of you walk and agree. Then you will experience the goodness of God when he sends you his best to love you. It's not God's will that you pay for love, because his love hung on a tree for you. His love awakens you every day, his love never gives up on you when you make mistakes, and his love does not judge you. His love covers a multitude of sins. God bless you, daughter! God's love never fails or quits!

THOUGHT PAGE

THOUGHT PAGE

_____

_____

_____

_____

_____

_____

_____

_____

_____

_____

_____

_____

_____

_____

_____

_____

_____

_____

_____

_____

My Driver Is Having Too Many Issues

As Forrest Gump stated, "Life is like a box of chocolates: you never know what you're going to get." This is a true statement if you don't trust God. Love is walking into a place of the unknown and trusting a person in whom you believe. Likewise, with God you walk with him, and you love him and trust him with all you have. In return God gives you the blessings of his kingdom. He gives you access to his treasures, and he trusts you with them. Contrast that to man. The words *love* and *trust* put fear in some of us. However, God loves us so much that he trusts us when we don't trust him.

When we get married, we do it because of many different reasons, but when it is for God, we do it for two reasons: love and obedience to God. In spite of why others do it, we do it because we love that person and our commitment to obey God. Marriage is valuable to God and is a great honor in his kingdom. Marriage is welcome in the presence of God. A marriage will have issues and mistakes, but God will restore it because he is patient and loves us. This is what we must remember when a spouse has issues. God has his love, and he is patient for us to get it right.

May I minister to you? There is no way you can please God if you decide to throw in the towel on your ordained marriage. What made you think your marriage would be fairy-tale perfect? What made you think your marriage would not be tested, tried, and proven? How were you going to get the testimony without a test? Did you come into the marriage without any baggage?

This man that you once called *husband* has gained other names—like worthless, cheap, deadbeat, lazy, sorry, and unsaved. This is a man you knew and loved in your heart, knowing that God chose him for you. Now he is going through changes in his life, but you don't want to endure? In other words, you do not want a prayer life, because his issues will keep you on your face. This is where love and patience come into the picture. You may think, *You're so right. I may not know what his issue is, but God does.* It's your job to pray for your driver. How is it you don't want to pray for your driver so that you both can enter into a place in God? He is your legal driver, and although his condition has changed in his life, it does not disqualify him. What if he is strung out on drugs now? God is more powerful than any addiction. The breaking power of this devil may rest in your belly, and yet you want to walk away because it appears your girlfriend's life is better than yours. Where in the Bible does it declare that you can divorce on the grounds of a spouse being on drugs? If you get in your place in the Spirit, you will find that drugs are the symptom, not the issue. The fact is that you have to be willing to fight for the soul of your spouse and not let the devil have him.

One thing you must remember is that when you got married, you were not perfect either. Your driver had to endure your past and the grudges you carried daily in your heart. He stayed and endured with you, and he stayed in the face of God. When you threw your tantrum in the car, he kept driving to make sure you arrived in the presence of God on time. Although you were yelling at him and screaming at the top of your lungs about how your life is so messed up, he kept praying. This behavior is a distraction while driving, but when you have God in your life, you look past the foolishness and pray. How dare you have the audacity to want out now that the tables are turned. Stop acting like a little girl, put on your big-girl panties, and pray for your husband. As a woman of God, it is your duty to pray for him, not for you to say, "Move over and let me drive!" Let God be God and work on the car; you simply have a flat tire and not a blowout.

When your driver has issues, you have to find out what needs to be fixed in the Spirit. One thing you must realize is that according to the Bible, we do not wrestle against flesh and blood. Whatever the spirit is, it does not recognize God, and once you step in the flesh and cuss out your driver, he becomes even further away from God. Now you have put yourself in trouble with God, because he is not looking at the one who stumbled—he's looking at the one who caused him to stumble.

Finally, you must realize that the issues cannot overtake your marriage. You defeat the devil with your love and patience, and most of all your prayers and commitment to God. In your marriage it may be deeper than just drugs, but you have to hear God in your decision to leave your marriage. God delivered you, and he will deliver your driver too.

God knew we all would have issues, and he definitely knew that marriage would have issues. It was always the plan of God for man and woman to become one. Marriage is valuable, and every day that you are married adds value to it.

THOUGHT PAGE

THOUGHT PAGE

Stop Kicking My Car

People today still do what people did long ago when it comes to cars that don't work right. They sometimes kick them because they are angry or because they are placed in a frustrating situation. Have you ever gotten out and kicked your car because it quit and did not start? Then you take it to be serviced, and now you have a dent that makes the car look bad on the outside. Now you are more frustrated because the look of the car is damaged. The fact is that the car cannot kick you back. All it can do is sit there and take the abuse. It can only change its appearance because of the damage that has been placed upon it. The car is weak when it comes to the person controlling it.

Likewise, a woman is weak when it comes to a man. A woman is not just physically weak; she is sometimes emotionally, mentally, and spiritually weak. There are some strong women in the world. However, I am talking about the weak-willed and silly women who are supposed to be saved, those who settle on having a man in their beds at night. Trust me—there are plenty out there.

As a woman, you cannot let a man beat you down and say he loves you at the same time. A man mentally beating you is worse than being beaten physically. Some women are helpless when it comes to abuse because they have the fear of man and not the fear of God. One may think that as the writer I am judging you; however, that is not true. That's how the enemy works: he sets up his prey and puts fear in them. Although there is fear, one has to find the strength to say, "Enough is enough." Men who hit women are weak and are not real men. Nothing in the Bible says you have to be his punching bag or his sex slave, that you have to be demeaned and ashamed. Nowhere in the Bible does it say to lie down and be his mat. A woman is supposed to honor her husband, love him, and help him. There is no reason to be kicked on and abused for the sake of a little boy trying to feel like a man.

Nevertheless, the women who think age is nothing but a number seem to get their doors beat in—and they embrace it. How do you let a kid beat on your car? "But I love him, and he loves me." Christ did not beat the Church; he loved and embraced it. How is it that as women, we allow ourselves to become so desperate? We settle for any kind of abuse that we think is love. A man who tears up your car—which means your house, children's lives, finances, ministry, and your relationship with God—is not worth keeping.

There are women who fight back but in the wrong way. Women have to learn to fight in the Spirit so that they will have certain victory. Declare as the woman with the issue of blood did: "If I touch hem of his garment, I shall be made whole."(Matthew 9:21 KJV) Likewise, you should declare that enough is enough, and when God brings you out of this, you are not going back. Tell the devil, "Stop kicking my car!"

Woman, you are worthy of a man's love, but you are more worthy of God. If you have the Holy Ghost, you are never alone. God is the kind of God who loves you. Let me paraphrase the Word of God in Isaiah 54. He makes it clear that he is the Lord thy maker, and he is your husband. He let you do what you want to do for a season without anger. He just hid his face in order to not see the disgrace you were placing upon yourself. He could not watch you indulge yourself in sin while trying to make a man love you who did not love himself. He could not watch you prostitute yourself to pay some bills. Let's clarify prostitution. If you exchange sex for any kind of gift from a man, *it is prostitution.* Therefore if he takes you to McDonald's and buys a cheeseburger from the dollar menu, and you go home and sleep with him, it's prostitution. You just prostituted from the dollar menu, but it's still prostitution. That man is not your husband, woman at the well. I am trying to help you before you lie with another man who is not your husband. God declares that he will take you back unto him and build you of rubies and stones. Therefore when the enemy comes again, it will not be from him. No weapon that forms against you shall prosper. This clearly means when you find your way back to God, he is still going to take you back and rebuild the woman again. When you are hurt and broken, that unsaved man cannot help you, but God's love never quits.

Don't think about that man whom God did not choose for your life. Let him go on because he is not your assignment. Serve the devil notice that he will not keep kicking your car. If your husband is beating on your car and he is saved, call the Holy Ghost to arrest him right where he is. His hand should only rise up to praise God, not to hit you.

THOUGHT PAGE

THOUGHT PAGE

Unwanted Passengers!

In marriages there are often many issues. When there is a disagreement, the driver cannot focus when he is being yelled at and being reminded of how stupid you think he is. That's why it is important to learn to agree to disagree. Whatever is going on within the car needs to stay in the car. When one of you makes a mistake, you must learn to love each other to a place of wholeness. Within the car you will find many valuables that have to be protected. A marriage it consists of five people the day you say I do. There is God, the husband, the wife, the little boy in him, and the little girl in her. When she throws a tantrum and the little girl comes out, he has to deal with that spirit. When the little boy shows up, she has to know how to pray. A woman can never change a man by conversation; she can change him by demonstration, because once he sees the God in her, he can recognize the God in himself.

There are unwanted passengers that come within the man or the woman in the marriage, if they are not delivered from their past. These passengers live in their hearts, spirits, and minds because of hurt that may have been imposed on them. The people can be baby daddies or baby mamas, or people with whom they had relations. Relations before a marriage is dangerous because you have no rights to anything and are putting your soul at risk for temporary feelings. Premarital sex causes emotions to scatter all over the place for one, but it may not mean anything to the other. When these soul ties are not dealt with, then when marriage takes place, there are two people standing at the altar, but there are many others standing within them. However, as it relates to the husband, if he marries a damaged woman, it will be very difficult to drive her where she needs to be in God, because she does not trust anyone. Deliverance needs to take place in order to obtain a successful marriage. Often in marriage people are taught to leave a person's past where it is, but the past is *important* so that mistakes will not be repeated.

Consequently, the car sometimes has unwanted passengers that distract the driver. These unwanted passengers are invited in the midst of anger, rage, tears, misunderstanding, miscommunication, and distrust. These unwanted passengers will not get out the car and start walking. They may have been invited in during the emotional times in the marriage. That is why you cannot confide in everyone about what is going on in your marriage.

The driver is being distracted by all these people who have crammed themselves in his car. Likewise, the passenger can't read the Word to the driver because the unwanted passengers are screaming out their opinions. The driver is distracted and driving all over the place; every time he turns around, unwanted passengers are telling him about his business. The unwanted passengers are rejoicing because they feel they have power over the marriage with their opinions. He has become a man who can't drive because of all the distractions in the marriage. The driver is going one direction, and the passenger is going in another. This means the car is all over the place, with two people fighting in the flesh instead of fighting for their marriage in the Spirit. The Bible declares in Genesis 2:24 KJV, "Therefore, shall a man leave his mother and his father and shall cleave unto his wife and they shall be one flesh." This means oneness in a marriage. When people talk about your spouse, they talk about you too. For example, if someone calls your husband stupid, they are also calling you stupid.

A married couple should never allow anyone to speak against their spouse. The unwanted passengers need to get out. The driver and passenger have to open up the doors and put those unwanted passengers out on the curb. Understand that you are both responsible for them riding around with you. If the unwanted passengers do not want to be in your lives because you both choose to be on one accord, then let them keep walking. The load has been too heavy and hard to tote around. The best thing in a marriage is when the load is light.

The Lord has been so good, because when confusion starts and no one can focus, he is the steering wheel that guides the car. When the car (marriage) is all over the road, God is still protecting it from a wreck. God stops the car from wrecking because he will not allow his plan to be voided.

When you know there are unwanted passengers in the car, stop and kick them out. A marriage can be destroyed by outsiders, and the man can't drive because of distractions and confusion.

THOUGHT PAGE

THOUGHT PAGE

Check the Gauges!

This chapter is for the driver of the car God gave to you. There are gauges in front of you on the dashboard of the car. As a driver, you are the one who sees them head-on. There is a seatbelt gauge to let you know that everyone in the car is safe; if it keeps making a sound, it means either the driver or the passenger is unsecure. If your oil light is on, you need find out where your oil is going. Ask yourself who you are pouring your oil into other than your wife. Lastly, if your temperature gauge is leaning toward the hot temperature, then you need to check what is going on. Don't ignore your gauges in your marriage. When that "check engine" light comes on, it means just what it says: check the engine. There are warning signs before the problem becomes an even bigger problem. If your wife tells you something is bothering her, check the engine. If she makes certain statements about the marriage, listen to the tone in her voice. For example, "I feel like you don't love me like you used to." Or, "I feel like we have lost our fire. You don't spend any time with me." Or, "I feel lonely although I am married." These are signs that the engine light is on, and you need to make some repairs.

Many times we ignore the gauges on our natural cars, saying to ourselves, "I'll fix it later because I really don't have the time or money to fix it now." We do the same thing in marriage when we ignore the warning signs that something is out of control. The temperature gauge is back and forth as long as the wife is unstable in her marriage. For instance, she is happy and full of life one day, and the next day she is mad at the world. The temperature gauge is going from cold to hot and not stopping in the middle. When a car overheats for a long time, it can blow a gasket and be destroyed. Then there are options presented to replace the motor, which means it will be a long process of healing or rebuilding the motor; that means the marriage has to be broken all the way down and rebuilt. Then the final option is to junk the car, which means the marriage is over.

One might think junking the car would be easier than investing in it. But when you love someone who is worth the investment, you do what is necessary to make the marriage run good as new. If you junk it, you leave it where it is, and someone else will pick up what you declared junk and rebuild it again. Just like a female dummy is ready to jump in the front seat and act like a wife, there is a male dummy ready to drive your family.

In a marriage, as the driver, you are given a mandate by God to take care of your family. Love your wife as Christ loved the church—this is a commandment, not an option. When you neglect your natural car, it will not run properly, and you can't go to where you need to go. It's the same way in marriage: when it is broken, you cannot take it where it needs to go. In a marriage where there is damage to the motor, it needs to be repaired immediately. Get your oil changed regularly by getting in the presence of God and allowing him to pour out the old oil and give your car fresh oil. Make sure you are not pouring into everyone else and abandoning your wife. Make time for her, and listen to her heart. Search for the root of the situation and not the symptom. In other words, don't look at her attitude to find out why she has an attitude. If you have an attitude and she has an attitude, then who's praying?

Water in a marriage is so important because it stops it from overheating. It puts out fires that the devil starts quickly, when you have God right in the middle of the marriage. The next time it gets heated in your house, shout, "Water!" That means, "God, I need you right now." Then open up your spirit and let God minister to you and give you directions. Your wife will let you drive her anywhere when she feels secure and knows that if the car has issues, those issues will be repairable and she will not be abandoned. If you watch the gauges and fix the car immediately, God will take care of you.

THOUGHT PAGE

THOUGHT PAGE

A Letter from the Author

My dearest brothers and sisters in Christ,

Reading this book myself, it reminds me of my past and how I had to mature and grow. I value marriage. There are no perfect marriages, and everyone makes mistakes. My testimony is that I was married to a thug, and I knew God, but my husband was familiar to my flesh because we had nothing in the Spirit. I was mistreated and dogged out. I had to learn to forgive him and move forward. We became good friends, and I quickly realized that he was not my assignment. I was holding on to my sister-in-Christ husband. It was never the plan of God for us to be together. I wanted him and he wanted me, and there was nothing spiritual about it. I created the mess in my life by ignoring the spirit and running after flesh. I tore him down with my mouth because I didn't know how to build him up. I was so focused on his downfalls that I could not see anything good in him. The Word of God declares, "A wise woman buildeth her house, but a foolish woman tear it down with her hands (Proverbs 14:1 KJV)". I was a foolish woman to my heart. I would listen to everybody about what I should do about my marriage.

In 2006 I remarried, and it was to a minister. In my mind I thought, *This is it.* We both were people pleasers, and we invited people in our marriage that were hard to get out. As a matter of fact, some of them never left until we were divorced. I had been so hurt that I had given up on marriage, but he was not my assignment either. We didn't get to know each other because of other people. When God joins two people in marriage together, no one can separate them. Once I forgave, I waited on God because I was tired of going in circles. My husband couldn't drive because of unwanted passengers in the marriage.

In 2012 I married my current husband, and he taught me how to let him love me. Then I realized that God loved me through him. My husband loves God, and he is an awesome pastor. He taught me that I am his first ministry, and he has to attend to my needs first. If I am broken or hurt, he can feel it in his spirit. I can deny that something is going on, but he checks his gauges by observing my body language and feeling my spirit. He reacts immediately and will not leave the room without a response and peace in his spirit. We agree to disagree without screaming and hollering. Trust me—at one time that was how we expressed ourselves. God stepped in and immediately changed it because we loved being married. In our obedience, God gave us a baby boy, my husband's first child. We're still praising God. I thank God for the Blessed Man Working in the Kingdom of God.

I learned to stay in the passenger seat and let him drive. I read the Word and encourage him, and when I feel his light is becoming dim, I pray the virtue back into him and ask God to restore his strength. This man is driving me toward my destiny. I relax in the Word of God and know that I am in good hands.

The other men who were in my life were not my assignments. There was good in them, but it was not my duty to bring it out of them. Everyone deserves to be happy, and happiness starts within you. In every woman's life, at some point she is with a man who can't drive. Sometimes he can't lead, and other times she won't let him drive. Either way, he is a man who cannot drive.

Acknowledgments

To my king, Wendell Pugh—I thank God that you found me in the midst of the garden. Many nights you labored with me when I was kicking and screaming about my past, ministry, and purpose. My king, you are amazing in all you do, and I am grateful that you are my greatest intercessor. I love you as my pastor, best friend, lover, and husband.

I would like to thank the entire Burning Bush family for all your support. To my family, who has encouraged me in all I do, I love you. To my children, Ni-angel, Dra-Quan, Ariel, Lyric, and Matthias—you are all my greatest inspirations. To my sisters, Sandra, Evon, Patricia, and Cathy, you all are wonderful women in my life, and I am grateful. Of course to my baby sister Latasha Kelly who looks up to me, I love you and thank you for calling and encouraging me in every area of my life. To Sabria Hemingway, you are my mother and I thank God for you. To Santain Pugh, you are one amazing woman as well, and I truly love you.

A few more special people in my life, Lachanda Salvage, Chekesha Mcgee, Mechelle, Corinthian Corruthers, Gwen Goodman, Triesure Dixon, Gloria Parker and Erika Jenkins. I thank you for sharing your life with me. You encouraged, cried and rejoiced with me. Thank you for a never ending friendship that God has joined together.

The key to a successful marriage is
God, love, trust, honesty
and understanding.

Printed in the United States
by IngramSpark

Printed in the United States
By Bookmasters